# Nordic

T0372279

# Style

BRAUN

# Chris van Uffelen

# Nordic

# Style

Warm &
Welcoming
Scandinavian
Interiors

# Contents

6    Introduction
7

8    Mylla Cabin
11  Mork-Ulnes Architects

12  Pedersen Residence
15  Baulhús

16  House M-M
19  Tuomas Siitonen Office

20  Øvre Tomtegate 7
23  Link Arkitektur

24  House Krokholmen
27  Tham & Videgård Arkitekter

28  Fredericia Furniture
29  Furniture

30  Langgata 13
33  Austigard Arkitektur

34  Stormvillan
39  Mer Arkkitehdit

40  The Roof House
43  Sigurd Larsen

44  Villa Sivakka
49  Architectural Office Louekari

50  Villa W
53  Wingårdhs

54  V-Lodge
57  Reiulf Ramstad Architects

58  Moebe
61  Furniture

62  Hadar's House
65  Asante Architecture & Design

66  House H
69  Hirvilammi Architects

70  Garbo Interiors
73  Design

74  K21 Skardsøya
77  Tyin Tegnestue Architects

78  Villa Arkö
81  Marge Architects

82  Forest House
87  Primus Architect

88  House of Many-Worlds
91  Austigard Arkitektur

92  House Husarö
95  Tham & Videgård Arkitekter

96  Normann Copenhagen
99  Furniture

100  Dikehaugen 12 "Sponhuset"
103  Arkitekt August Schmidt

| 104 | Villa Torö |
| 109 | Trigueiros Architecture |

| 110 | Farm House Dalaker/Galta |
| 113 | Knut Hjeltnes Sivilarkitekter |

| 114 | House K |
| 117 | Hirvilammi Architects |

| 118 | Slävik |
| 121 | Fahlander Arkitekter |

| 122 | Mountain Cabin at Lisetra |
| 125 | Pushak |

| 126 | Margrethe Odgaard |
| 127 | Rugs |

| 128 | The House in the Thicket |
| 131 | Kasper Bonna Lundgaard |

| 132 | Archipelago House |
| 137 | Trigueiros Architecture |

| 138 | PH House |
| 141 | Norm Architects |

| 142 | The Tervahovi Silos |
| 145 | Pave Architects |

| 146 | Single Family House Hoffstad |
| 149 | Knut Hjeltnes Sivilarkitekter |

| 150 | BoConcept |
| 153 | Furniture |

| 154 | Gray House |
| 157 | Pushak |

| 158 | Villa Kristina |
| 163 | Wingårdhs |

| 164 | Gjøvik House |
| 167 | Norm Architects |

| 168 | Studio Tolvanen |
| 171 | Furniture |

| 172 | Malangen |
| 177 | Stinessen Arkitektur |

| 178 | House Y |
| 181 | Arkkitehtitoimisto Teemu Pirinen |

| 182 | Summer House Gravråk Addition |
| 187 | Carl-Viggo Hølmebakk Arkitektkontor |

| 188 | Index |
| 190 | |

| 191 | Picture Credits |

# Introduction

Nordic style essentially includes Scandinavian design and architecture, but a strict geographical definition would only cover Norway and Sweden, as well as the northwesternmost part of Finland. The rest of Finland would be missing, as would Denmark, while the Russian Kola would be added. Nordic style is therefore defined more culturally and historically and also includes Iceland, the Faroe Islands, the Åland Islands and, ultimately, Greenland.

Architects of the first half of the 20th century laid the foundation for Nordic style that was to overcome the national romantic styles: Kaare Klint, Alvar Aalto and Arne Jacobsen. With the exhibition "Design in Scandinavia" at the Brooklyn Museum in 1954, which was shown for three years throughout North America and found successors in other countries, not only did Scandinavian design become popular, but the term "design" also turned into a worldwide marketing concept for contemporary goods, shifting from craftsmanship to industrial production. Scandinavian designs, minimalist, functional and in discreet colors, were produced and sold worldwide from now on. In Scandinavia it was the Lunning Prize that since 1951 has contributed to the development of the awareness and quality of the Nordic style. When the prize was discontinued in 1970, the acme of this design also passed. In the 1970s, the Scandinavian building boom ended and IKEA adopted the idea of affordable "democratic design" in its own way to temporarily promote furniture as a non-durable item. In conflict with the local industry, the company had already previously relocated its production to cheaper countries and in the 1980s increasingly focused on inexpensive products. In the 1990s and 2000s, Nordic style was completely out of fashion – until the second decade of the 21st century celebrated its comeback. The furniture of the first wave of Scandinavian design has become a classic inspiring a young generation of designers, and the ecological architecture of the Nordic countries has always served as a role model. This book shows how to live comfortably in this relaxed Nordic style.

# Mylla
# Cabin

a

**Architect**
Mork-Ulnes Architects

**Location**
Jevnaker County,
Norway

**Gross floor area**
84 m²

**Year**
2017

**Material**
Heart pine, ore-pine (Pinus sylvestris),
pine plywood with lye and white oil
finishing

Mylla sits firmly on a hilltop and is shaped by the forces of the surrounding landscape. Though planning regulations required a gable roof, the dwelling divides the gable in half to create four shed roofs radiating in a pinwheel configuration. Two sheltered outdoor spaces are created which are protected from the wind and from snow shedding from the roof. The exterior is kept simple and clad with untreated heartwood pine planks that will weather over time. The compact interior, finished in plywood and combined with a continuous roof canopy, can house up to ten people across three dedicated bedrooms and fully-equipped bathrooms. Custom plywood furniture, including bed frames, bunk beds, couch, dining table, benches, and shelves characterize the interior.

## Jevnaker

b

c

The comfortable dining area.

Ground floor plan.

Exterior view with the surrounding forest.

Spacious openings enhance the re-lationship to the environment.

The interior is determined by bright pine wood.

Bedroom in soft tones and minimalist design.

a

# Pedersen
# Residence

Architect
Baulhús

Location
Flateyri, Ísafjarðarbær,
Iceland

Gross floor area
250 m²

Year
In progress

Material
Wood

This abandoned house had been empty for 15 years when it
aroused Halfdan Pedersen's interest. The designer and his
friends demolished and rebuilt it from ground up, using strictly
reclaimed and salvaged materials from all over Iceland. All visible wooden elements, walls, floors and ceilings were personally
collected by the architect throughout the country. Every door
and every cabinet, sink, faucet, bathtub, radiator – and every-
thing in between – was found, cleaned, restored, transported
and assembled piece by piece, even the corrugated iron facing
on the outer walls and roof. Following a sustainable approach,
the massive recycling project has taken 13 years of careful and
patient work and is still ongoing.

Flateyri

a
Upstairs living room.

b
Bright surfaces contrast the dark
wooden elements.

c
Fireplace and work desk.

d
Open staircase with carpet.

e
Comfortable loft napping nook.

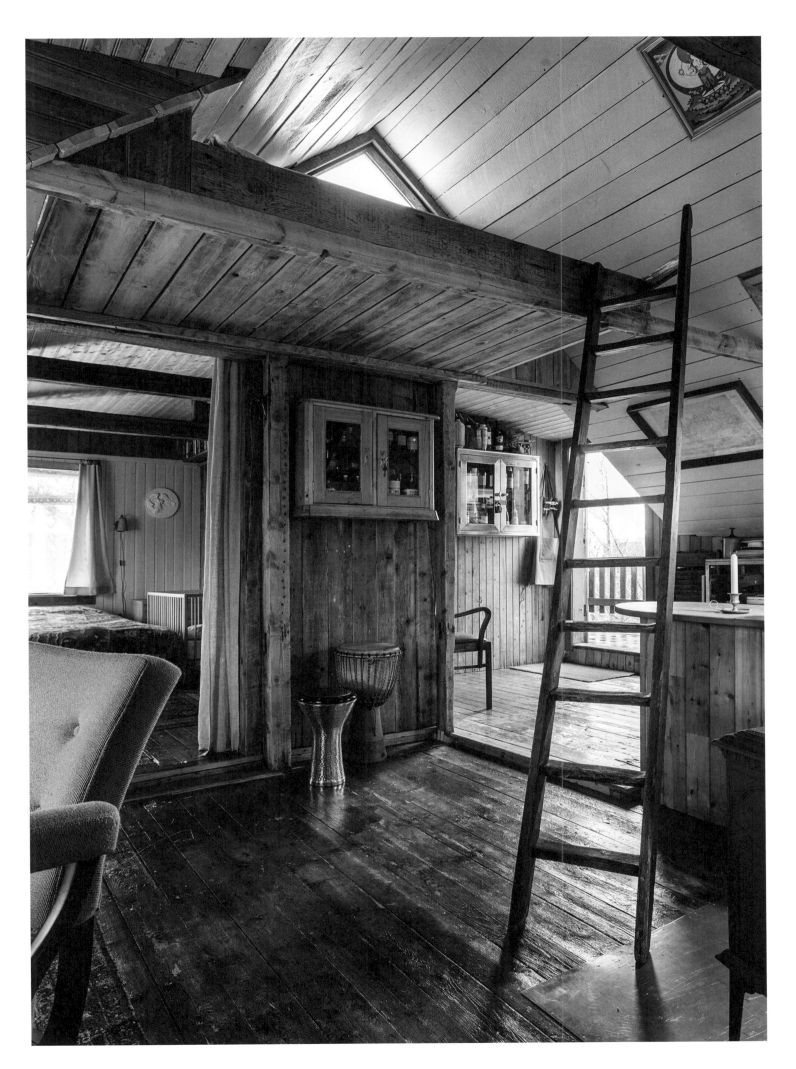

# House
# M-M

a

**Architect**
Tuomas Siitonen Office

**Location**
Helsinki,
Finland

**Gross floor area**
170 m²

**Year**
2013

**Material**
Wood frame, Siberian larch cladding

The new home was designed with two apartments. The lower story is a level-access studio apartment for a 91-year-old grandmother. The ground floor also includes sauna and utility spaces. The 100-square-meter apartment upstairs is the home of a couple and their teenage children. Upstairs there is also a large reception room and a kitchen, made to measure in flamed birch, that serve as the whole family's living space. In summer this extends effortlessly outdoors via a large terrace. The three-story building sits comfortably on the slope, the large windows bring in the greenery and create the feeling of a tree house. The exterior of Siberian larch changes with the seasons and will gradually turn gray, while the interior is a mixture of subtle colors and accessories inspired by nature.

# Helsinki

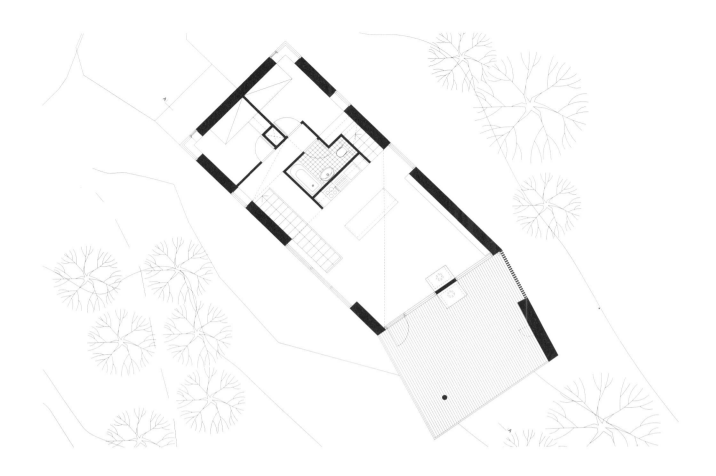

e

f

a
The loft character enhances the airy impression.

b
The dwelling is strictly related to its environment.

c
Several spacious areas offer an opportunity to meet and enjoy family life.

d
In summer House M-M extends outdoors via a large terrace.

e
First floor plan.

f
By using mostly wood a sustainable approach was chosen.

# Øvre Tomtegate 7

a

**Architect**
Link Arkitektur

**Location**
Sellebakk, Borge,
Norway

**Gross floor areal**
149 m²

**Year**
2015

**Materials**
Kebony wood, aluminum and glass

Inspired by the original design of the 19th century, a run-down farmhouse was brought into the 21st century. The design of the new building was strongly influenced by the traditional gable roof farmhouse and the surrounding landscape. Glass and aluminum were used extensively. Both the roof and the façade of the extension are clad in Kebony, chosen by the architects to preserve the traditional style of the original farmhouse. Exposed to sunlight, Kebony changes its original dark brown color to a soft silver-gray patina. The interior creates a visual contrast to the traditional exterior through light surfaces and a minimalist design language. Openings up to the ceiling serve as a link between these two design concepts.

b

c

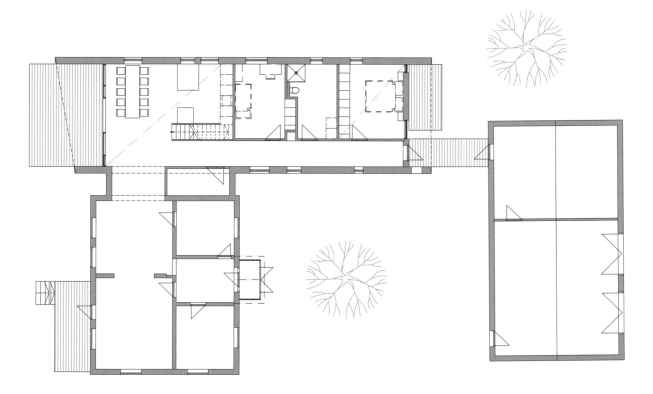

d

a
Kitchen with bright surfaces and mini-malist design.

b
The building opens to the nearby garden.

c
White colored furniture and acces-sories enhance the contrast to the wood-clad exterior.

d
Ground floor plan.

e
The construction is inspired by the traditional farmhouse.

f
The long stretched form helps to organize the different units.

e

# Värmdö

# House Krokholmen

Architect
Tham & Videgård Arkitekter

Location
Krokholmen, Värmdö, Stockholm
archipelago, Sweden

Gross floor area
135 m²

Year
2015

Material
Cedar and ash wood, zinc, steel

The plot of House Krokholmen on the relatively small island of Krokholmen in Stockholm's outer archipelago benefits from open views and it is at times exposed to strong winds. The family wanted a maintenance-free vacation home in one level with social space both inside and outside. The large family room with kitchen and entrance faces out towards the sea with daylight and view in three directions. A central wall holding the fireplace gives access to bedrooms, bath and storage that are oriented to the forest in the west. The living room opens up through large sliding doors onto three terraces. The horizontal openness of the main space out towards the sea is balanced by its verticality, an internal ridge height of six meters in the unifying arcuate roof. Curved glulam beams rest on the low gable façades and meet along a ridge roof beam. The tent-like room and silhouette of the house connects to the idea of the least complicated way to spend time in nature, but it is also inspired by the older Swedish pavilion – and gazebo architecture, light buildings carefully placed in the landscape. A screen of wood and glass runs around the house and unites interior and exterior spaces on a base of in-situ cast concrete.

a
Living room with large window seen
from the coast.

b
Looking in the opposite direction,
the living room rises to a height of six
meters.

c
The living room with a protective side
terrace, seen from the kitchen.

d
Interior wall panels and carpentry are
made of ash wood.

e
Kitchen on one side of the living room.

f
Screen of wood seen through the
windswept dwarf pines.

g
Floor plan.

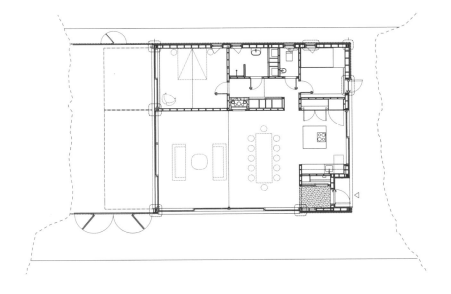

# Fredericia Furniture
## Fredericia

**Products**
Trinidad, Pato 4 Leg Center

**Location**
Fredericia,
Denmark

**Established**
1911

**Favorite materials**
Solid wood, premium leather

Fredericia began as a thoroughly Danish design house. From the very beginning, one of the main focuses was the dedication to the perfection and further development of the design craft. Simple principles determine the designs that are created as the modern originals of tomorrow. Simple principles that reward outstanding quality through careful material selection, functionality and attention to detail. Fredericia cooperates with a carefully selected group of international designers, all renowned for their exceptional design integrity. The claim to create contemporary design that is always beautifully finished, relevant and esthetically fascinating is the guiding principle and driving force behind all products of the Danish design company.

Stavanger

# Langgata 13

**Architect**
Austigard Arkitektur

**Location**
Langgata 13, Stavanger,
Norway

**Gross floor area**
80 m²

**Year**
2015

**Material**
Birch veneer

The interior spaces of this house for Storhaug Utvikling are sculpted to form a varied sequence of spaces, with emphasis on the changes between light and dark spaces as well as between open and intimate spaces. In a small house it is also important to pay attention to all the small "bonus" spaces, such as window sills for sitting in. The interior is all wood, ranging from dark pine floors to light beech walls. The house has utilized regular building methods easily available, and despite its high material and spatial quality it is completed at a normal building cost. In Scandinavia, too, the two main concepts of housing construction in the second half of the 20th century – detached houses on large plots in suburbia, and on the other side, large-scale housing schemes – did not lead to success. This calls for a revival of the small-scale, high-density, Nordic urban house typology. In the town of Stavanger, this house alone has attracted a lot of attention, and is now spurring a revitalized focus on this typology, in politicians, bureaucrats and developers.

d

e

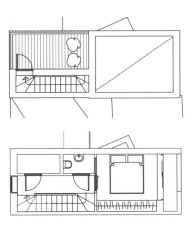

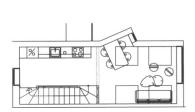

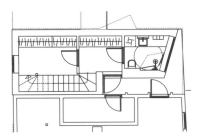

f

a
Living room on the second floor.

b
Historical pattern with metropolitan density.

c
Stairs leading to the roof terrace.

d
The staircase.

e
Small-scale individual building.

f
From below to above: ground, first, second floor
and terrace plan.

# Stormvillan

a

**Architect**
Mer Arkkitehdit

**Location**
Hanko,
Finland

**Gross floor area**
239 m²

**Year**
2016

**Material**
Façades: spruce, render (ground floor)
Roof: zinc

Situated in the historic villa district of Hanko, Stormvillan not only creates a strong relationship to the historic value but also to the surrounding landscape. The ground floor cuts into the rock and the villa is entered on beach level. At the very end of the ground floor is a room with two walls of bare bedrock, the wine cellar. A carpet clad staircase leads up to the main floor. Designed as a home for an elderly couple, the villa also has an elevator and fully accessible bathrooms. The main floor is all about light, views and flowing space. By using spruce cladding and traditional linseed oil paint the ensemble pays homage to the nearby 19th-century villas. The roof of the ground floor level serves as a wooden terrace with a section of green roof. The zinc roof blends into the coastal hues of the sky.

# Hanko

a
A contemporary interior with bright surfaces and warm tones.

b
Exterior view at night.

c
Spacious openings enhance natural lighting.

d
Floating interim between living and dining area.

e
A dynamic interplay with the roughness of the surrounding landscape.

f
Rustic wine cellar.

g
The ground floor cuts into the nearby rocks.

h
Floor plan.

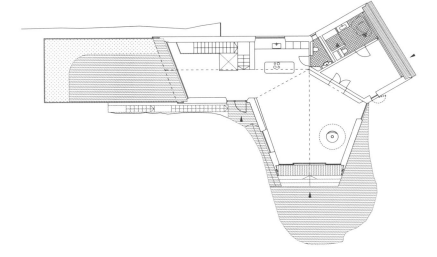

# The Roof House

Architect
Sigurd Larsen

Location
Copenhagen,
Denmark

Gross floor area
150 m²

Year
2016

Material
Untreated larch wood, concrete floor

Natural light is an essential element when building in the Nordic countries. Indirect light has a beautiful cold blue color that is reminiscent of the proximity to the ocean. The low sun from the south adds a warmer yellow light to the spectrum. The Roof House is designed to catch both and turn it into an ever-changing experience when walking through the sequence of rooms. The house is crowned by a roof of sloped surfaces. A perforated wall circumferes the house and creates different grades of privacy and windless outdoor spaces. From an open court the entrance is located right at the heart of the dwelling. From here, high ceilings open up to a spacious living room. The kitchen is directly connected to a southeastern court offering morning sun. A series of customized furniture completes the airy and elegant impression.

Copenhagen

c

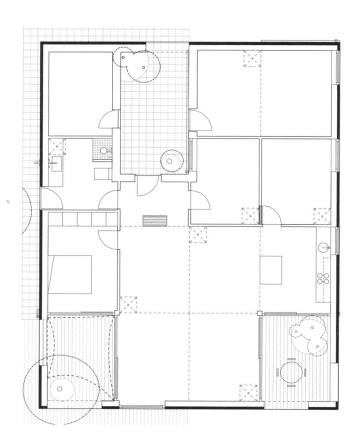

d

a
The sloped roof surfaces function as organization feature.

b
Bright surfaces and concrete flooring create a timeless impression.

c
Customized furniture functions as visual contrast.

d
Ground floor plan.

e
The kitchen is directly connected to a light-flooded court.

# Villa Sivakka

## Muonio

b

Architect
Architectural Office Louekari

Location
Lake Äkäsjärvi, Muonio,
Finland

Gross floor area
48 m²

Year
2015

Material
Wood

Villa Sivakka is a small log house located on the shore of Lake Äkäsjärvi in Muonio, Lapland. The house is designed for a family that has lived on the plot for half a century – it is their holiday home. 205 millimeters thick logs were used and the outside walls are protected with boarding, which is tarred on the sides. The house consists of main living room/kitchen, two sleeping rooms, bathroom and hallway. On the upper floor there is additional space for two people to sleep. In the middle of the living room there is a stove, which can supply an important part of the heat needed in winter. A characteristic part of the interior is the large bay window overlooking the lake and the mountains. Wood can be found throughout the whole building, giving the ensemble a comfortable and unpretentious impression. The building is surrounded by large forests, some of which are protected and have the status of a national park.

a
The most popular place in the villa is the sofa in the bay window.

b
View from the upper level to the living room/kitchen area.

c
The large window offers spacious views to the nearby lake.

d
All small sleeping units are connected to the living room.

e
The log house blends harmoniously into the surrounding landscape.

f
Ground floor plan.

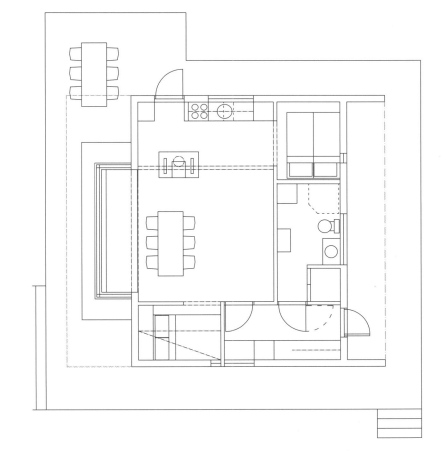

# Villa W

Architect
Wingårdhs

Location
Kungsbacka,
Sweden

Gross floor area
750 m²

Year
2012

Material
Concrete, slate from Penhryn, Wales,
Corian

The villa on the west coast of Sweden was built for a client who collects art and design objects of various kinds. In order to offer the collections independent space, seven independent wings were erected, which also serve different living functions: entrance, view, dining, cooking, relaxing or for the accommodation of guests. The interior is strictly white to show the objects to their best advantage. The exterior, on the other hand, is covered with black slate – polished on the façades, irregular on the sides, which plays with the sunlight with its different surfaces. The numerous roof terraces are intended to house a sculpture collection.

a
All rooms have their own view of the landscape.

b
The staircase that swings down, made entirely of white Corian.

c
The freestanding staircase looks like a sculpture in space.

d
The grand piano, specially painted in Ferrari-red, and view towards the lake.

e
Ground floor plan.

f
The center of the building with all the rooms, wings and views.

g
First floor plan.

h
Site plan.

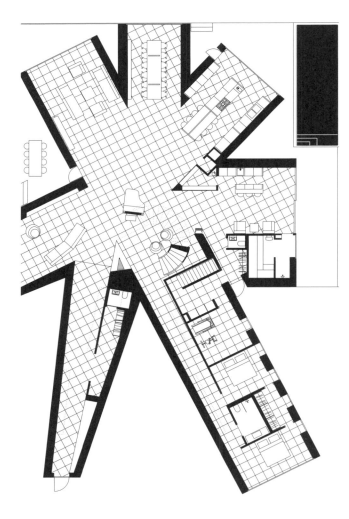

f

g

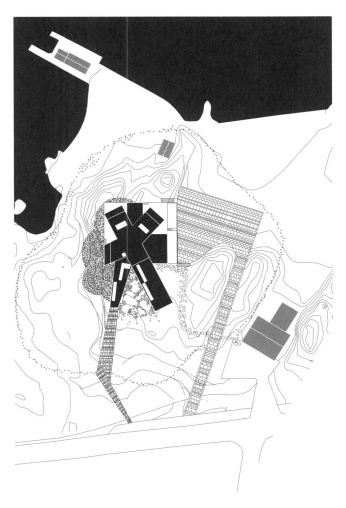

h

# V-Lodge

a

**Architect**
Reiulf Ramstad Architects

**Location**
Buskerud,
Norway

**Gross floor area**
120 m²

**Year**
2013

**Material**
Bare plywood and in-situ concrete

This all-year cabin is carefully placed on a slight slope, where the volume creates small microclimate zones with beneficial sun conditions for outdoor activities and easy access from the inside. The building consists of two bodies united in a V-shaped plan. The interior is simple but refined: walls, ceiling and solid furniture are clad in bare plywood, and the combined fireplace and kitchen unit is cast in-situ concrete. Glazed openings from floor to ceiling provide sufficient daylight. A comfortable seating niche serves as an ideal place for relaxation. Each bedroom is accessible through sliding doors along a narrow corridor with steps that go down with the terrain and lead to a youth lounge overlooking the glazed gable end.

Buskerud

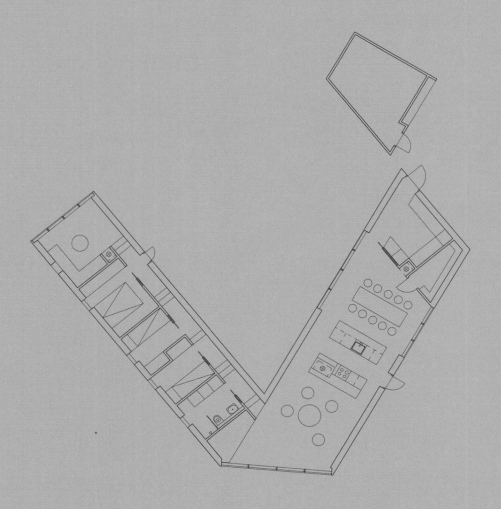

Dining area, kitchen and living room are united in a spacious open space.

Openings from floor to ceiling enhance the connection to the exterior.

The use of wood in the entire design reflects the connection with nature and sustainability.

Ground floor plan.

Bright plywood can be found throughout the whole structure.

The comfortable niche serves as refined place for relaxation.

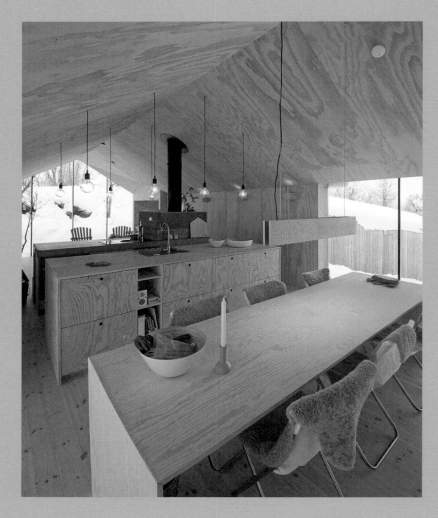

e

# Moebe

a

## Products
Side Table, Coat Rack, Shelving System, Wall Hook, Frame

## Location
Copenhagen, Denmark

## Established
2014

## Favorite materials
Locally sourced wood, especially oak, brass

Moebe is a Scandinavian design brand based in Copenhagen. The design company was founded in 2014 by cabinetmaker Anders Thams and architects Nicholas Oldroyd and Martin D. Christensen, with a goal to create clean and beautiful designs that surprise in their simplicity. Moebe's designs are therefore often constructed based on solutions that in an architectural way bring together more than one element and material without gluing, welding or any other hidden solutions. This way of constructing requires great precision and focus on details. A Moebe-design can thus always be recognized by its minimalist and clean esthetic expression and by the surprisingly simple and clear formal language.

b

Copenhagen

c

a
Side Table is designed to be able to move at a moment's notice and is assembled without any welding gluing or sticking.

b
Coat Rack is a subtle rack with a simple expression and is equipped with pegs that can be moved around as needed.

c
Shelving System can be built as tall, wide and with any angle you like. Wedges hold the shelves in place, letting you place them at any height.

d
Wall Hook has two points for hanging. As the actual hook points inwards, its form is closed and very harmonious.

e
Frame has a free and fully transparent center, as the construction is kept to the outer edge, held together by a rubber band.

d

# Hadar's House

a

**Architect**
Asante Architecture & Design

**Location**
Stokkøya, Åfjord,
Norway

**Gross floor area**
60 m²

**Year**
2015

**Material**
Wood, Shou Sugi Ban wood

The house is part of the project Bygda 2.0, a rural development project on the island of Stokkøya that focuses on developing modern Norwegian houses into a dynamic village. The house is separated into two units and partly based on wooden pillars to meet the topographic conditions. Wooden panels with different treatments offer a variety of colors for the interior. Floor tiles enhance the entrance and the bathroom floor. The bathtub is clad with the same tiles as the ones used for the bathroom floor. It is submerged into the floor to allow an undisturbed view of the nature outside giving a feeling of stepping right into the land-scape. The trapezoidal metal sheets of the interior roof are left exposed and form a playful contrast to the warm wood as they reflect the light from the sky and the water into the building.

Stokkøya

c

d

64
65

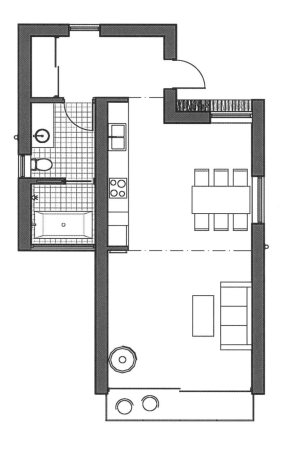

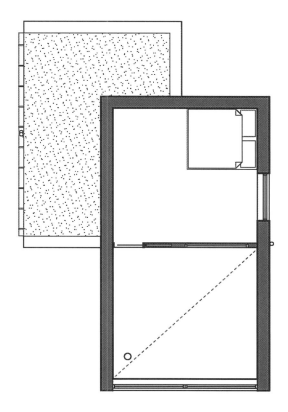

a
Dining area surrounded by bright surfaces.

b
Simple but playful entrance area.

c
Kitchen with color contrasts.

d
Limited furniture allows the landscape to become part of the room.

e
Ground and upper floor plan.

f
Bathroom with sunken tub and view of the Norwegian Sea.

a

# House H

**Architect**
Hirvilammi Architects

**Location**
Seinäjoki,
Finland

**Gross floor area**
204 m²

**Year**
2014

**Material**
Radially sawed spruce wood

House H was built for the architect's own family. The narrowness of the plot and its wedged shape influenced the shape of the house and its location. The materials were chosen to suit the environment and to integrate the new ensemble harmoniously. The house consists of the main building and an annex. Somewhat contrary to convention, the bedrooms and utility room were placed on the ground floor and the living room on the upper floor to enjoy the views to the surrounding landscape. The annex houses a study and guest room as well as a wood-heated sauna. The interior is characterized by bright spruce surfaces, accompanied by light-colored furniture and accessories. By involving local material suppliers and builders, the project focuses on high-quality craftmanship, combining Finnish tradition and contemporary lifestyle to create a link between old and new.

# Seinäjoki

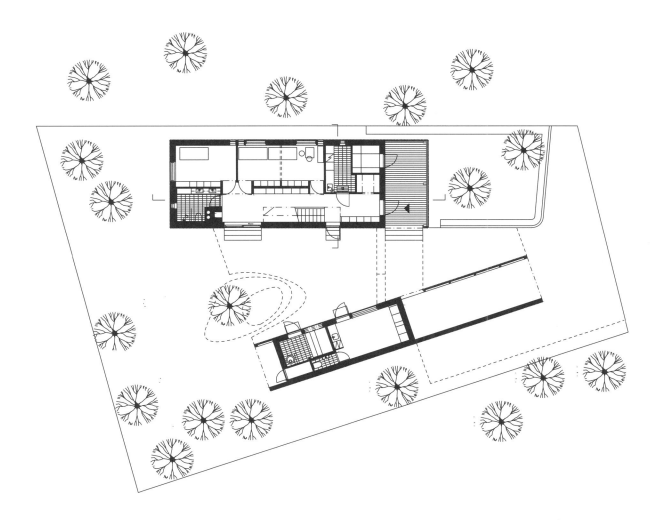

e

a
The interior is determined by bright spruce surfaces.

b
Living room with spacious openings.

c
Bedroom in soft tones located on the ground floor.

d
The dark exterior functions as visual contrast.

e
Ground floor plan.

f
Living and dining room located on the first floor.

# Garbo Interiors
## Lidingö

Products
French and Swedish antiques intermixed
with contemporary pieces

Location
Lidingö,
Sweden

Established
2003

Favorite materials
Natural linen, wood and stone

Luxury is not in gold and glitter but in the raw material. Natural linens, wood and stone materials – these are the guiding aspects for Garbo Interiors. A mixture of antiques, contemporary and modern trend pieces as accents give the designs a sophisticated and individual touch. Over time, the natural materials change in color and texture, creating a dynamic environment that changes as do the people who live in it. The aim of the Swedish design company is to focus on the natural beauty of the raw materials, creating environments that combine contemporary design and craftsmanship into a comfortable yet stylish ensemble.

a
A practical shelf for high ceilings with ladder to reach and space to display clothes, books or objects.

b
Antique benches mixed with vintage in a seating area with modern sofa and antique bergerees.

c
Hallway with old pressed flower pictures and modern lighting.

d
Kitchen with Calacatta marble and French vintage furniture.

e
Garbo round mirror with Swedish antique chest of drawers.

# K21
# Skardsøya

a

**Architect**
Tyin Tegnestue Architects

**Location**
Møre og Romsdal,
Norway

**Gross floor area**
60 m²

**Year**
2016

**Material**
Untreated spruce

This cottage combines important aspects of Norwegian cultural history with the amenities of a modern living space. The structure is modest in size and is surrounded by marshland, rocks close to the sea and scattered pine and juniper vegetation. The main building is a stud house with beamed ceilings on three different levels. Most of the construction work was carried out by the owners themselves. The outside of the building is covered with spruce, which was harvested from the clients' own forest. The interior is dominated by light wood and soft tones that contrast the roughness of the surrounding nature and adapt the principles of traditional Norwegian design to combine them with contemporary eye-catchers.

# Møre og Romsdal

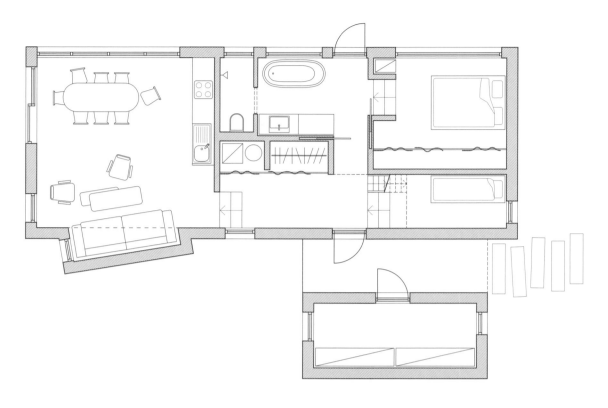

d
Ground floor plan.

a
Kitchenette with wooden surroundings.

b
Living area determined by Norwegian design tradition and contemporary style.

c
Even in the bathroom the surrounding landscape can be enjoyed.

d
Ground floor plan.

e
Wood and soft tones create a sense of comfort and warmth.

f
The cozy interior provides an unobtrusive setting to enjoy the rough beauty of the Norwegian countryside.

# Villa Arkö

**Architect**
Marge Architects

**Location**
Arkö, Norrköping archipelago,
Sweden

**Gross floor area**
200 m²

**Year**
2012

**Material**
Sedum

Balancing on top of a steep, rocky slope facing the water, the gripping view of the landscape was a natural starting point for Villa Arkö, a small summer residence situated on an island in the Norrköping archipelago. Conceived as an archetypical Swedish summer house, the building is organized around three main components – the cottage, the insulated veranda, and the outdoor terraces. The three volumes seem to descend the slope, simultaneously mimicking and accentuating it. Clad in cedar panel that will weather into gray (the veranda roof in lush green sedum), the materials used are all chosen for their sustainability and esthetic qualities. As they age, the building will slowly blend with the surrounding archipelago – a mass amongst many in this landscape of blues, greens and grays.

Norrköping

e

a
The living room with large windows.

b
A ladder leads to the upper floor.

c
The freestanding fireplace.

d
Steps to the garden.

e
The building stands on a slope.

f
Ground floor plan.

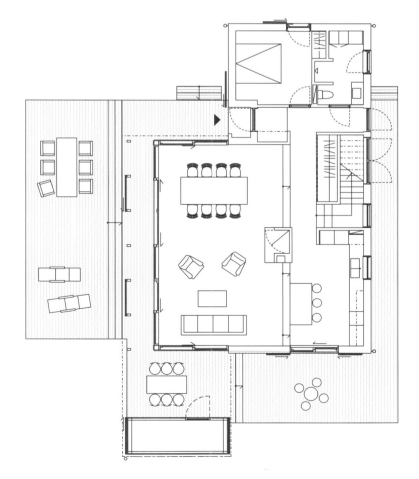

f

# Forest
# House

**Architect**
Primus Architect

**Location**
Asserbo, Zealand,
Denmark

**Year**
2014

**Material**
Wood, concrete floors

The project is located at a long, slender plot facing the edge of a forest. The clients wanted to shut the house off to the adjacent buildings in order to have an exclusive experience of the forest. One aim was to create a spatial setting for large dinner parties as well as a space offering intimacy. The façade is a lapped cladding in solid oak boards treated with iron sulfate, which protects the wood and creates the weathered surface. The furnishing of the interior is created by the skewing of the plan, which offers hidden storage space and a hidden entrance covered by oak panels. A polished concrete floor accompanies the built-in heating interior walls made of wooden boards of slightly different thickness, creating a tactile surface that captures the light.

Zealand

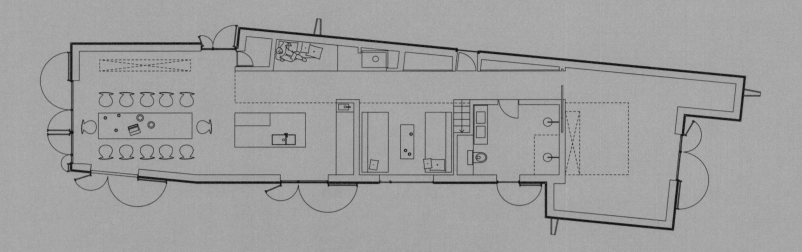

f

a
Dining area with view to the forest.

b
The concrete flooring contrasts with bright surfaces.

c
Geometric forms and wooden elements merge to create a contemporary living environment.

d
Bright walls with tactile surface.

e
Corridor running along different zones.

f
Ground floor plan.

g
Wooden furnishings function as vivid contrasts.

h
The layout allows for maximal height and natural lighting.

g

# House of Many-Worlds

a

**Architect**
Austigard Arkitektur

**Location**
Kleivveien 68, Bekkestua, Bærum,
Norway

**Gross floor area**
100 m²

**Year**
2018

**Material**
Birch veneer, perforated steel plates

A large family table forms the center of the apartment. Here you have a great view into nature, where squirrels and birds frequently show up. The large table allows different activities to be carried out at the same time. From this family table towards the interior, space becomes progressively intimate, with kitchen, lounge and library forming individual zones in a continuous social situation without separate rooms. The loft forms the most intimate zone of the apartment. Protected by half-transparent perforated steel panels on either side, one can have a complete overview of the social situation straight below, as well as the exterior beyond that.

## Bærum

a
The family table measuring 1.5 × 3.0 meters.

b
The house in the Oslo region.

c
In the loft.

d
Library with buillt-in furniture.

e
View from the loft to the table.

f
View from the table into nature.

g
From below to above: ground floor and loft plan.

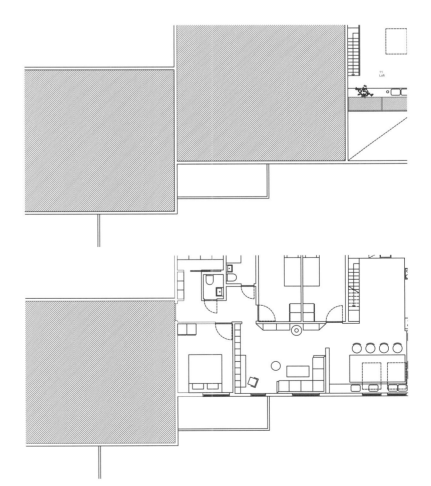

# House Husarö

**Architect**
Tham & Videgård Arkitekter

**Location**
Österåker, Stockholm archipelago,
Sweden

**Gross floor area**
180 m²

**Year**
2012

**Material**
Plywood, glued laminated timber, black
sheet metal

The house is placed on a plateau facing the sea in the north, which has long been owned by the family. The pitched roof house is entirely clad with folded black sheet metal of varied widths that integrate the position of the windows. Three glazed sliding doors with frames of hard wood provide entrances and direct access to the outdoor areas on the naturally flat part of the bedrock. Within the square plan, a freestanding box holding kitchen, bathroom and the staircase organizes the social area on the ground floor into a sequence of interconnected spaces. Large sliding windows open up to the views in all directions and allow the sunlight to fill the interior. On the upper level, with bedrooms and a playroom, a skylight that runs along the ridge of the roof underscores the verticality of space and subtly enhances the experience of seclusion.

# Österåker

92
93

c

d

a
Front door and kitchen seen through
the window.

b
View to the dining table from outside.

c
The skylight in the pitched roof.

d
Beds beneath the skylight.

e
The living room with vaults bent between glued laminated timber beams.

f
Sections.

e

f

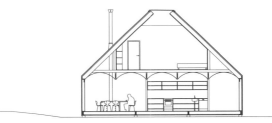

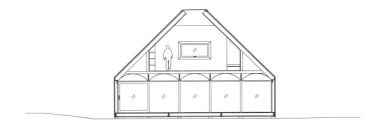

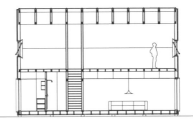

a

# Normann Copenhagen

**Products**
Swell 3 Seater Sofa, Solid Coffee Table, Pad Lounge Chair, Slice Dining Table, Hyg Lounge Chair Swivel, Journal Desk

**Location**
Copenhagen, Denmark

**Year**
1999

Normann Copenhagen is a Danish design company, founded in 1999 by Jan Andersen and Poul Madsen. In 2012, an in-house design studio was established. In addition to the internal team, Normann Copenhagen cooperates with external designers from all over the world. The designers' work focuses on high-end designs for everyday pleasure, whether in a residential setting, at work or at leisure. The products are shaped by curiosity and enthusiasm. Driven by joy and excitement of great design, high-quality products are created, crafted with great attention to detail, materials, craftsmanship and durability, thus being an enriching contribution to contemporary lifestyle and personal well-being.

Copenhagen

a
The soft curves of the Swell 3 Seater Sofa appear elegant and yet comfortable.

b
Soft tones make this lounge chair suitable for every living room.

c
Slice Table can be transformed according to the client's individual wish.

d
Hyg Lounge Chair Swivel is a mixture of esthetics and pragmatism.

e
Journal Desk is suitable for a comfortable work experience.

d

# Dikehaugen 12
# "Sponhuset"

a

**Architect**
Arkitekt August Schmidt

**Location**
Dikehaugen 12, Vaadan, Trondheim,
Norway

**Gross floor area**
125 m²

**Year**
2015

**Material**
Pine wood

Dikehaugen 12 or "Shingle-house", built for August Schmidt, is a small one-family home situated amid trees in the outskirts of the city of Trondheim, Norway. The complex comprises three saddle-roof built volumes: dwelling, sauna and annex, all constructed in wood and clad with pine shingles. The residential is energy efficient and environmentally sustainable. Although the house is compact, a flexible floor plan allows for much living space. The materials are natural and the construction is breathing. The building is low-maintenance, the exterior surfaces are unpainted and allowed to age with the weather. Indoor surfaces are also made of untreated wood which does not require surface treatment. The robust design of the complex, the flexible layout and the building volumes aim at being distinct, but well-tuned to the immediate natural surroundings.

Trondheim

c

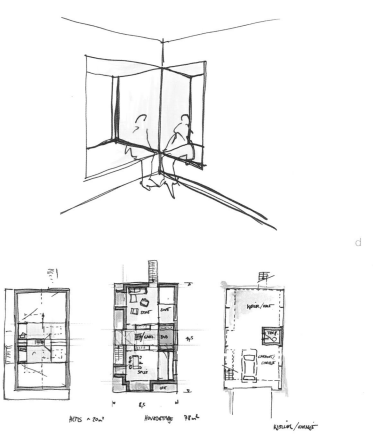

d

a
The kitchen with a movable wardrobe as room divider.

b
Main entrance with artificial light.

c
Wood and plant-based, recyclable materials at the main house and the annex.

d
Sketch of the bay windows and plans of the roof, the main and entrance floor.

e
Living room with skylight.

f
Seating niches in the dining room.

g
Wooden beams and shingles at the entrance to the living room.

h
Stairs between shingles and climate shell giving access from the main entrance to the main floor.

# Villa Torö

a

**Architect**
Trigueiros Architecture

**Location**
Torö Island, Nynäshamn,
Sweden

**Gross floor area**
280 m²

**Year**
2018

**Material**
Interior: oak, granite, Douglas fir, terazzo, linen, concrete, brass, brushed copper, glazed brick. Exterior: cedar panels, black aluminum windows, iron, concrete

The building is shaped and influenced to adjust to the site's materials; its rocks, minerals, pine forests and the ocean winds. The summer residence is located on a natural mountain ridge overlooking trees and the archipelago countryside. Despite its generous building volume, a small scale suitable for the terrain was created: different bodies are linked and materials are carefully selected to create a natural look. The ground level rooms are tailored to the needs of the hunting lodge and consist of durable materials and rustically carved furniture. The diagonal staircase leads up to main floor where natural light from generous windows and openings creates an atmosphere reminiscent of a forest clearing. The top floor is a private attic, with bespoke cabinets and customized bathroom with natural stones and niches facing the tree tops.

Nynäshamn

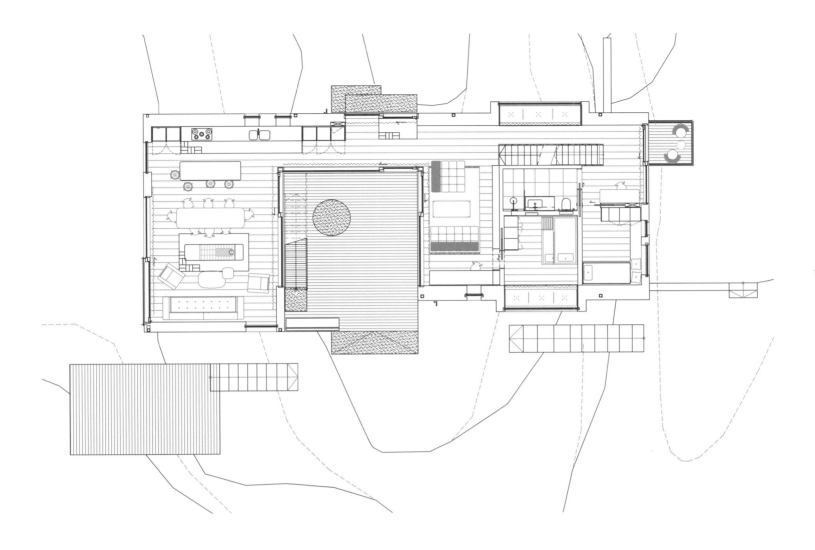

a
Entrance area surrounded by forest.

b
Top floor private attic in the tree tops with a distinct shaped roof.

c
The interior in calm natural colors.

d
Ground level space with furniture in rustic, durable materials.

e
A serene living room in the middle of the forest.

f
Floor plan of the main level.

g
Traditional kitchen with different elegant tinted colors.

# Farm House Dalaker/Galta

a

**Architect**
Knut Hjeltnes Sivilarkitekter

**Location**
Rennesøy, Rogaland,
Norway

**Year**
2013

**Material**
Prefabricated solid wood (spruce),
fiber-cement boards

This new farmhouse for Turi Dalaker and Tom Galta is placed 150 meters from the old farm buildings so as not to disturb the completed cluster of the farmstead. The house utilizes an old pigsty as a foundation. The ground floor plan is simple, a cross in the middle of the rectangle provides space for storage, bathroom and entrance. Crosswise the core is slightly offset to make the kitchen and living room deeper. The plan offers users different movement patterns despite its modest size. The building is highly prefabricated, using solid wood technology for floor, lateral walls and roof. The prefabricated wood remains in its natural state, thus creating an interplay of warm tones. The cores are conventionally built and painted black. In 2013 an extension with two bedrooms for the children and an additional living room completed the ensemble.

# Rogaland

d

e

f

a
The house is raised above the ground to leave the landscape as untouched as possible.

b
Raised ceiling in the dining area.

c
A spacious opening in the living room reinforces the visual connection to the surroundings.

d
Living room with black, lacquered surface, natural wood cladding and stove.

e
Additional bedroom in the annex.

f
Ground floor plan.

# House K

## Seinäjoki

b

**Architect**
Hirvilammi Architects

**Location**
Seinäjoki,
Finland

**Gross floor area**
180 m²

**Year**
2016

**Material**
Cross-laminated timber

House K was designed for a friend of the architect. It is situated on a slope near a forest. In order to improve the connection to the landscape, the position of the openings was carefully chosen. Stretched over two stories, the ensemble consists of entry, bedrooms, utility rooms, sauna, a library corridor and a kitchen and dining. The living room was designed as an additional pavilion to the courtyard and the pine forest. The main material is cross-laminated timber (CLT). The project was carried out in close cooperation with the Finnish timber company Crosslam and served as a research project for the investigation of finely tuned visible CLT interior surfaces. By combining the latest technologies of the wood industry with the cultural knowledge of craftmanship, House K is both – a bow to the Finnish building tradition and a contemporary design solution.

a
Light colors create a minimalist
impression.

b
The openings were carefully placed
to enhance the connection between
interior and exterior.

c
Cross-laminated timber was chosen as
main material.

d
Exterior view with the nearby forest.

e
Ground floor plan.

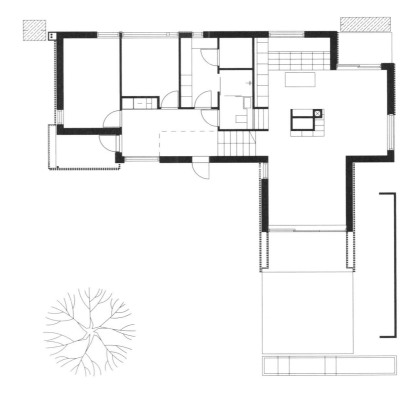

a

# Slävik

Architect
Fahlander Arkitekter

Location
Slävik on Härnäset, Bohuslän,
Sweden

Year
2011

Material
Corrugated fiber cement board, untreated fir, galvanized steel, glulam

The summer house is located between two fjords on the Swedish northern west coast. The site is surrounded by a national park characterized by rounded granite rocks and windswept trees. Located on one of the highest points in the area, the house hovers lightly above the ground. A room for socializing, cooking and eating fronts the ocean, with large sliding windows towards the expansive view. The climate contrasts typical for this region determines the design. Entrance hall, bedrooms and bathroom are placed at the back. An extra bedroom and a sauna are located in a nearby guesthouse. The interiors of the house are completely covered with panels of untreated fir. When the interior walls are set alight by the low sun from the west, the house becomes a glowing eye-catcher from the ocean.

b

Bohuslän

c

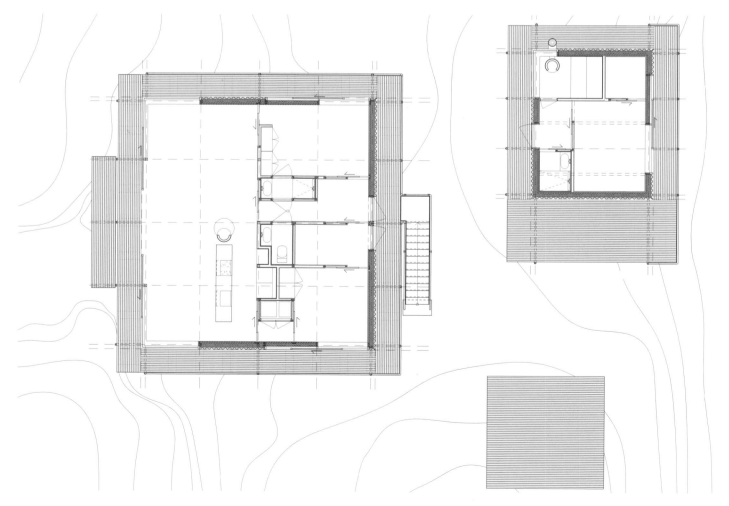

d

e

a
The living room opens to the
surrounding landscape.

b
Untreated wood is used throughout
the interior of the house.

c
The house seems to hover above the
ground.

d
Ground floor plan.

e
A mixture of traditional materials and
contemporary esthetics.

# Mountain Cabin at Lisetra

Architect
Pushak

Location
Hafjell, Øyer,
Norway

Gross floor area
100 m²

Year
2014

Material
Pine, concrete

The low, elongated shape of the cabin is inspired by traditional mountain farm buildings, but a modern mountain cabin is a place for friends and family to gather. Hence this project is planned around several spaces for spending time together, but also with a variety of secluded areas for privacy. From every room, even from the bathtub, there is a view to the landscapes and open sky. Outer walls and roof have shiplap cladding of local heartwood pine, and rain gutters are also wood. Interior floor, walls and ceiling are clad with knot-free, waxed pine boards. The wax doesn't seal the surface, and allows for the wood to achieve a natural patina. The kitchen floor is sanded concrete with exposed aggregate of river gravel, and the fireplace is cast on site. Two annexes have been built at a later stage, creating a sheltered yard and a sunny terrace.

Øyer

e

a
Sofa niche with view.

b
Kitchen and ladder to mezzanine.

c
Dining area towards lounge and fireplace.

d
Fireplace in front of lounge built into
the outer wall.

e
South façade with lounge bay.

f
Elevations, section and floor plan.

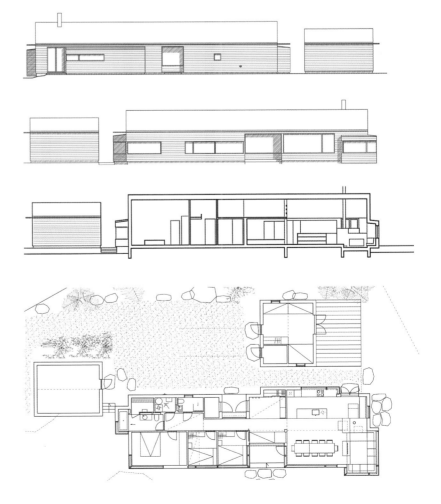

f

# Margrethe Odgaard

**Product**
Ply Rug for Muuto, Pebble Rug for Muuto

**Location**
Copenhagen, Denmark

**Established**
2013

**Favorite materials**
Wool, cotton, linen and silk

When entering the studio of Margrethe Odgaard, one is met by an abundance of light, colors and tactility. The airy loft reflects her mission: to develop designs that explore the feeling of colors and patterns in the physical environment. As a result of her dedicated work with color, Odgaard has developed several color indices that form the basis of her constant search for new compositions and tactile experiences. In 2016 she was awarded the prestigious Torsten & Wanja Söderberg Prize. Among other collections, her work can be seen in the collection of the Cooper-Hewitt Design Museum in New York. In addition to running her own studio, Odgaard designs furniture and objects as part of the duo Included Middle with furniture designer Chris L. Halstrøm.

Copenhagen

# The House in the Thicket

**Architect**
Kasper Bonna Lundgaard

**Location**
Hvasser Island, Færder, Norway

**Gross floor area**
244.4 m²

**Year**
2012

**Material**
Concrete, timber, wood fiber insulation, untreated pine boards, straight edged spruce boarding

The initial idea for this project for Britt Bonna Ringerike was to create a home that can exist both outdoors and indoors. During the summer, an atrium, a greenhouse and the nearby woods offer a strong connection to the surrounding landscape. During spring and fall, the greenhouse and atrium become an extension of the main house. The basic structure is divided into two parts: a private zone with bedrooms and bathroom, and a more public zone with kitchen and living room. The two parts are divided by a functional wall used for storage. As far as possible, all building materials are renewable and environmentally friendly. Wood was used wherever possible and the heating system is entirely based on firewood. The interior design is determined by different tones of wood which creates a vivid interplay of natural tones and shades as well as a warm ambience.

Færder

c

d

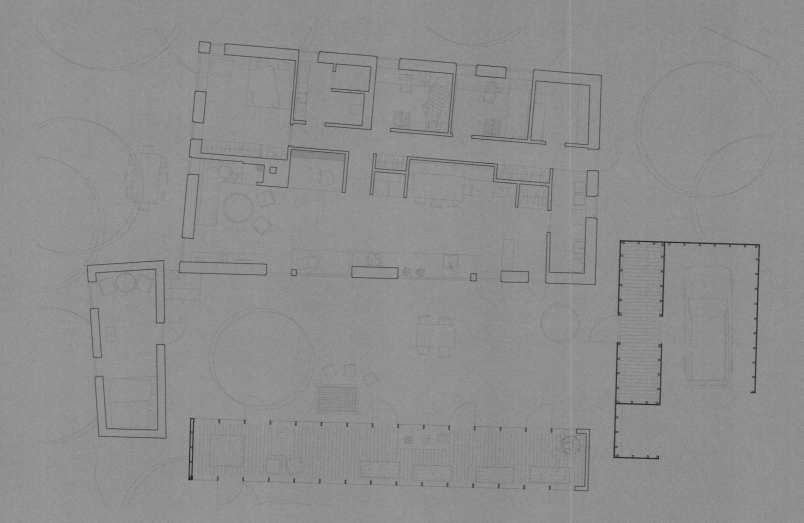

Kitchen and dining area.

The greenhouse as extension of the living context.

Living room with fireplace plastered with cement mortar.

The atrium functions as extension of the living environment.

Ground floor plan.

View to the atrium.

# Archipelago House

a

**Architect**
Trigueiros Architecture

**Location**
The High Coast, Ångermanland, Sweden

**Gross floor area**
95 m²

**Year**
2018

**Material**
Interior: Douglas fir floors, oak, leather, linen, glazed brick. Exterior: larch, bronze aluminum window frame and casing

Like a giant glacier, this simple larch panel–clad building sits in a crack in the exposed rock face of Sweden's northern coastline. Thick larch covers the façades of the cabins, the roof and the various terraces, accompanied by details of soft heat-treated ash, creating a versatile tactile experience. The interior reflects a more sensitive side, with calm, muted colors and materials housing smart and humble functions. Panel boards of wood, carefully brushed with pigment or linseed oil cover the walls while large solid wood boards lie on the floor. A local northern brick has been chosen for the floor and wall surrounding the fireplace at the heart of the cabin. Linen textiles in soft, warm colors and a distinctive selection of handcrafted Scandinavian furniture and international pieces complete the individual design.

Ångermanland

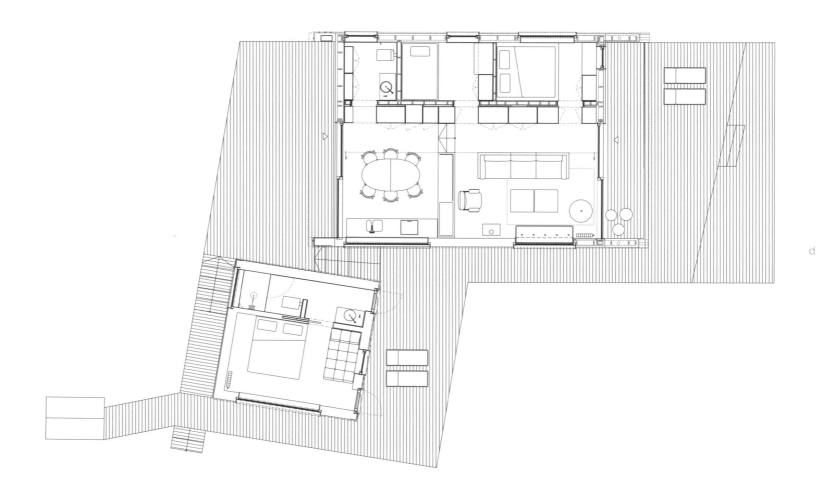

d

e

a
Dining area with natural lighting and numerous spotlights.

b
A place for reflection with view.

c
The living room with vertical division of social spaces.

d
Ground floor plan.

e
The filigree building floats above the massive bedrock.

f
Several openings create a strong relationship between interior and exterior.

g
Soft textures and muted colors in the bathroom.

# PH House
## Copenhagen

b

Architect
Norm Architects

Location
Copenhagen,
Denmark

Year
2018

Material
Wood, glass, teak, marble, concrete,
furniture and accessories by Menu

The villa, located in Copenhagen, is said to have been the home of the famous Danish design-icon Poul Henningsen. Today, a family of three resides in the historic house – a modern home that holds references to its original state – with beautiful high panels, parquet flooring, low, paned windows, teak furniture and – of course – retro PH lamps hanging over the kitchen island. The ground floor of the house has been changed from small divided rooms into one big living area with windows on all sides, only subdivided centrally by bespoke elements; a large kitchen cabinet covered in dark stained oak separating the kitchen and the living room, and a central staircase, creating a dynamic, semi-open space with soft transitions. The floating steps in solid oak create a flow between the basement, ground floor and top floor, connecting the house vertically in a harmonious and contemporary way with skylights increasing the sense of height and spaciousness.

d

e

a
Soft tones and dark furniture create a dynamic impression.

b
Bright surfaces and wood flooring enhance the impression of spaciousness.

c
The dark kitchen cabinet organizes the room structure.

d
Brass and gray ceramic stone combined to an elegant ensemble.

e
A simple formal language determines construction and furniture alike.

f
Teak and marble express a feeling of exclusivity without being exaggerated.

f

# The Tervahovi Silos

a

**Architect**
Pave Architects

**Location**
Oulu,
Finland

**Gross floor area**
10,805 m² (whole complex)

**Year**
2014

**Material**
Concrete and dark metal

A new life was breathed into the area of Toppilansalmi in Oulu, Finland, when the mid-century cylindrical grain silos, the landmark of the area, were transformed into a modern residential building. The round silos were used as balcony zones of different sizes. A predominantly rectangular dark extension expands the silo structure naturally within the newly conceived plot. The first two of 13 floors consist of new buildings with galleries, housing spacious, five-meter-high open living spaces. Adapting the original industrial atmosphere of the area, the raw in-situ concrete surfaces are a vivid element throughout the interior of the building. The combination of industrial design and contemporary solutions and materials creates a unique atmosphere.

## Oulu

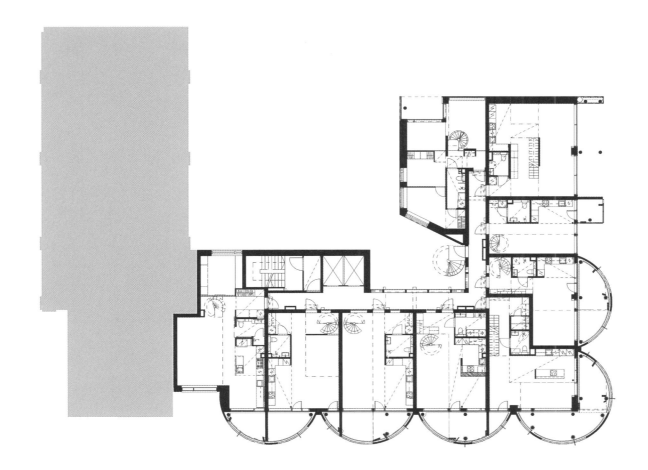

a
Uncovered concrete ceilings bear witness of the industrial history of the building.

b
Loft ground floor plan.

c
Wood contrasts the pragmatic industrial character.

d
Spacious living and dining area.

e
The former round shape of the silos can be found throughout the whole ensemble.

f
Exterior view at night.

# Single Family House Hoffstad

a

**Architect**
Knut Hjeltnes Sivilarkitekter

**Location**
Sandefjord, Vestfold,
Norway

**Gross floor area**
250.2 m²

**Year**
2012

**Material**
Prefabricated massive wood construction, fiber cement boards, pine plywood
boards

The project for Lene and Torbjørn Hoffstad is located on the
top of the Vesterøya peninsula and offers a view of the fjord to
the east and west. Due to the difficult topographical conditions
special care had to be taken with the outer skin of the house.
The lower part of the building consists of in-situ concrete,
the upper part is a prefabricated massive wood construction,
which runs as beams over the large opening of the ground
floor. The circular windows allow the openings in the walls to
become larger. By adapting the fiber-cement exterior cladding,
the garage and the northern wall of the entrance area function as connecting link between interior and exterior. The walls
of the lower part are clad with sand-colored fiber-cement
boards, which can be found in the bathrooms as well, thus en-
hancing the coherence of construction and interior design.

## Vestfold

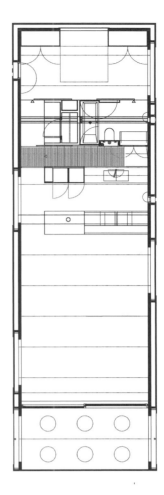

d

e

f

a
Open kitchen with fireplace and living space.

b
Dining area with circular windows as seen from
the entrance.

c
The spacious south window.

d
Work area with view of the surrounding landscape.

e
Upper floor plan.

f
Open kitchen, separated by a skylight that illumi-
nates the worktop.

a

# BoConcept

Products
Milano Table, Amsterdam Sofa, Carmo
Sofa, Adelaide Chair, Nantes Sofa,
Cupertino Desk

Location
Herning,
Denmark

Established
1952

Favorite materials
Wood, leather, felt, velvet and ceramics

BoConcept is the brand name of Denmark's most global retail furniture chain with 250 sales units in 60 countries around the world. Starting from a holistic approach the company focuses on the creation of customized, coordinated and affordable furniture and accessories. Following the client's request BoConcept offers esthetic, yet pragmatic design solutions. Elegance and high quality melt with Scandinavian minimalism to create dynamic living environments. By using wood and other natural materials the connection to traditional design elements is enhanced, while an individual form language and innovative structural solutions create ensembles suitable for the needs of a contemporary urban lifestyle.

Herning

e

f

a
Milano Dining Table is characterized by a geometric shape and slim wooden legs.

b
Amsterdam Sofa is determined by sharp lines and sweeping curves.

c
The modern Carmo Sofa is a real show-stopper with a cubic look.

d
The iconic Adelaide Chair is all about curves, comfort and character.

e
Soft and stylish, Nantes Sofa offers comfortable elegance.

f
Cupertino Desk combines workspace and storage.

# Gray House

## Oslo

**Architect**
Pushak

**Location**
Bygdøy, Oslo,
Norway

**Gross floor area**
380 m²

**Year**
2013

**Material**
Brick, concrete, slate, granite, wood

The clients – an older couple – wanted a home that was maintenance-free and without steps or thresholds on the main floor, situated in the garden of their former residence. Partially shaped so as not to hinder the view from the old house, the building is placed in a steep slope and surrounded by retaining walls that form terraces and paths. The interior is planned with emphasize on the view toward south and east, and on openness between the main living rooms. Floors and walls are site cast concrete, and all exterior materials are mineral; brick, concrete, slate and granite. The different gray tones in the exterior give a homogenous and solid impression, while the different material structures and patterns create a subtle variation.

a
Stairs, large window and lamp.

b
Dining table and fireplace.

c
Living room on the ground floor.

d
Bathroom.

e
Exterior.

f
Different levels and heights.

g
Basement, ground floor and first floor plan.

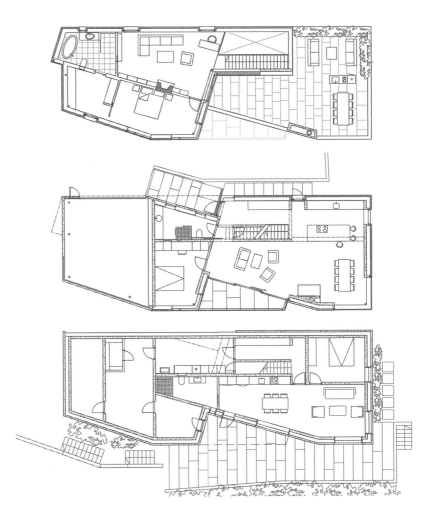

# Villa Kristina

a

**Architect**
Wingårdhs

**Location**
Gothenburg,
Sweden

**Gross floor area**
180 m²

**Year**
2014

**Material**
Silicone-treated softwood, whitewashed
spruce

The house for a young couple in the west of Gothenburg is surrounded by other detached houses. An atrium concept shifts the focus away from the neighborhood. It is open to the southwest with views of old trees and an exposed bedrock. The building is perched lightly on piers and stairs and a ramp along the blank northeast side leads up to the front door. The entrance wall is thickened to hold a fireplace – the chimney is part of the roof landscape – with a built-in sofa, a room for collections, the kitchen (back-to-back with the exterior mechanical room), and an air-lock entry with guest bathroom. A steep ladderway gives access to the study, where you can have a look at the sea. In the courtyard a shallow but almost monumental processional staircase leads up to a roof terrace.

# Gothenburg

a
The construction leaves the bedrock almost untouched.

b
The oblong house ends in a lookout tower.

c
A steep ladder illustrates the height of the tower.

d
The open kitchen with a 7.5-meter long table.

e
Ground and first floor plan.

f
The house has a closed perimeter, but a transparent inside.

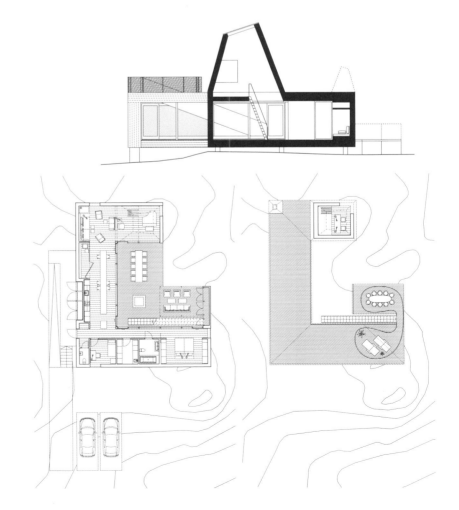

# Gjøvik House

a

**Architect**
Norm Architects

**Location**
Gjøvik, Oppland,
Norway

**Gross floor area**
155 m²

**Year**
2018

**Material**
Concrete, wood

The house gracefully embraces the hilly terrain, merging in a modest and natural way with its surroundings. Consisting of six cubes, overlapping each other in plan and section, a cozy universe filled with nooks and crannies was created. The interweaving of the different sections is underlined by the choice of materials. Concrete, wood and subtle, warm colors determine the design. The fact that the majority of the furniture is built-in contributes to the soft, yet minimal expression in this unique family home. Selected views are framed in windows spread out between the cubes, while the kitchen, being the heart and center of the house, offers a wider view, with light flowing through the room between the floor-to-ceiling windows on both sides.

Oppland

a
The façade cladding will blend with the surrounding landscape during the years.

b
Living room in concrete and soft tones.

c
Kitchen area.

d
Spacious openings enhance the connection to the environment.

e
The interplay between dark and bright surfaces evokes a dynamic impression.

f
Wood functions as warm contrast.

# Studio
# Tolvanen

b

Products
Visu Chairs and Base Table for Muuto, Julie Chair for Inno, Nakki Sofa for Wood, Hancock Baskets and Wood Hand for Furnishing Utopia

Location
Helsinki,
Finland

Established
2015

Favorite materials
Wood, recycled PET felt, extruded aluminum

Studio Tolvanen is the product design office of Mika and Julie Tolvanen. Mika is a Finnish designer who started his own practice after graduating from the Royal College of Art in 2001. Julie is an American designer who worked as a carpenter for ten years before moving to Finland in 2009 to complete a master's degree in furniture design. The starting point of their work is the belief that design should be determined by function, as this is the first purpose for each product. Nevertheless, Studio Tolvanen's products have an individual character, meeting the requirements of both – pragmatism and esthetics. According to the designers, a product should be understandable and self-explanatory, stand for itself and serve its purpose in a fresh and uncomplicated way.

# Helsinki

e

a
Visu Chairs were designed for Muuto.

b
Julie Chair was designed for Inno. Visu Chair and Base Table were designed for Muuto. Hancock Baskets and Wood Hand were designed for the Furnishing Utopia Exhibition.

c
Visu Bar Stool is a mixture of warm wood and elegant forms.

d
Nakki Sofa determines each living room with its unique character.

e
With its simple appearance Nakki Sofa adapts Scandinavian minimalism.

f
Plywood gives Visu Chair a warm appearance and robust flexibility.

f

# Malangen Peninsula

a

**Architect**
Stinessen Arkitektur

**Location**
Malangen Peninsula, Troms, Norway

**Gross floor area**
200 m²

**Year**
2017

**Material**
Cedar, oak, concrete, glass

The clients are a family with small children, and also wanted this place to give room for invitation of the larger family and friends. The conceptual layout was conceived as several individual volumes connected via in-between spaces and a central winter garden, placed on a natural shelf in the terrain. The organization provides both privacy and room for several activities at the same time. The central winter garden, with fireplace and outdoor kitchen, functions as the entrance to the building. A few steps lead down to the open space kitchen/living room overlooking the fiord and the afternoon sun to the west. A dedicated exit from the kitchen leads to the south-facing outdoor area where the family enjoys their dinners on warm summer days. The separation into volumes seeks to emphasize the transition between spaces and activities.

# Malangen

a
The fireplace in the living room.

b
Outlook between volumes.

c
Terraces towards the fiord.

d
The dining table.

e
View from above.

f
Ground floor plan.

g
Inside the central winter garden.

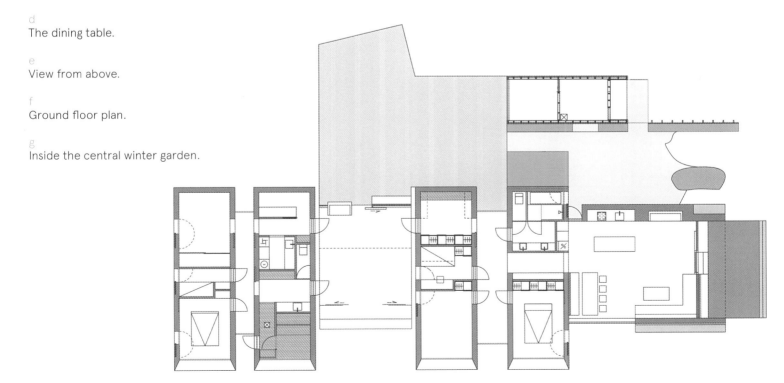

a

# House Y

Architect
Arkkitehtitoimisto Teemu Pirinen

Location
Iisalmi, Savonia,
Finland

Gross floor area
194 m²

Year
2016

Material
Siberian Tamarack, pine, spruce

The client wanted to restore the plot of this big and old-fashioned property to a natural pine forest, and built a small home, which fits completely into this landscape. The new building consists of three barns put together in a Y-shape. Each of the three wings has a different spatial scale to meet the individual functions and create a sense of hierarchy. The interiors are clad with a subtly whitened spruce to enhance the experience of the scenery. The concept of three interconnected wings and the extensive use of glass creates a spatial flow inside the house. The cell-like spaces of the bathrooms and bedrooms are introduced into the open interior space as boxes made of white plywood, reinforcing the illusion of a converted old barn. A large black fireplace acts as the centerpiece of the interior and as a traditional focal point.

Savonia

c

d

e

a
View from southeast at twilight.

b
The living room overlooking the surrounding countryside.

c
View into the distance and reflection
from the southern patio.

d
Master bedroom under the pointed
roof.

e
Kitchen and dining area with roofs
pointing in different directions.

f
Plan of the entire ensemble.

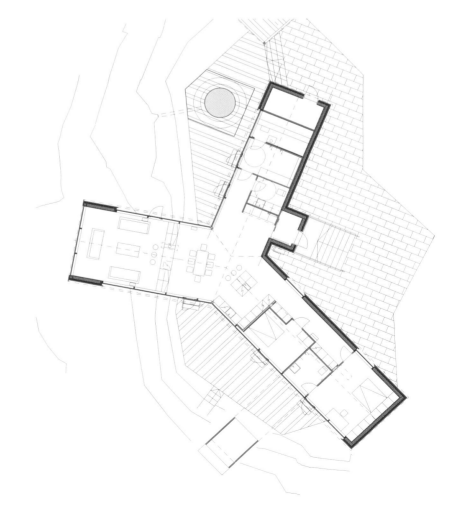

f

# Summer House Gravråk Addition

a

**Architect**
Carl-Viggo Hølmebakk Arkitektkontor

**Location**
Kuberget, Flakstad, Lofoten,
Norway

**Gross floor area**
25 m²

**Year**
2015

**Material**
Birch plywood, untreated spruce, zinc,
aluminum

The addition and rehabilitation to this "Nordlandshus", a traditional northern Norwegian house, is located on a remote site in the coastal island area of Lofoten. It re-uses the geometrical principle with asymmetrical dormer windows to let in light and give a view from the loft. The primary construction for the extension is prefabricated pine glulam. The interior is clad in birch plywood, while the exterior is clad in untreated spruce, which has grayed by sunlight and rain. The roof is clad in standing seam zinc roofing, and the windows have two-fold frames with aluminum in the exterior and wood in the interior. The climate in the area is quite extreme, especially with wind conditions in mind. While the old house is guy-wired to the ground, the extension is wind-anchored to the encapsulating concrete slab that acts as a stabilizing counterweight.

# Flakstad

c

d

a
Summer House Gravråk with old parts
to the left.

b
View into the kitchen from outside.

c
New entrance and fireplace.

d
View across the kitchen from outside.

e
View into the old part with open door.

f
View into the new part of the first
floor.

g
Sections and floor plans.

h
Kitchen, dining table and artwork by
Jan Håfstrøm.

e

f

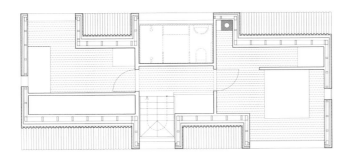

g

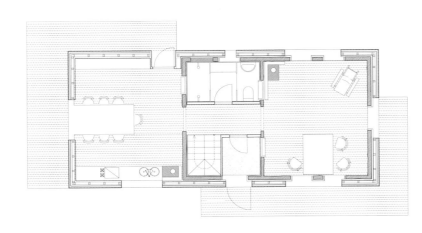

# Index

Asante Architecture & Design
www.asante.se
62

Austigard Arkitektur AS
www.austigard.no
30, 88

Baulhús
www.baulhus.com
12

BoConcept
www.boconcept.com
150

Fahlander Arkitekter
www.matsfahlander.com
118

Fredericia Furniture A/S
www.fredericia.com
28

Garbo Interiors
www.garbointeriors.com
70

Hirvilammi Architects
www.hirvilammi.archi
66, 114

Knut Hjeltnes Sivilarkitekter
www.hjeltnes.as
110, 146

Carl-Viggo Hølmebakk Arkitektkontor
www.holmebakk.no
182

Sigurd Larsen
www.sigurdlarsen.com
40

LINK Arkitektur
www.linkarkitektur.com
20

Architectural Office Louekari
www.arkkitehtitoimistolouekari.fi
44

Kasper Bonna Lundgaard
www.stillautvikling.no
128

Marge Architects
www.marge.se
78

Mer Arkkitehdit
www.merarkkitehdit.fi
34

MOEBE
www.moebe.dk
58

Norm Architects
www.normcph.com
138, 164

Normann Copenhagen
www.normann-copenhagen.com
96

Margrethe Odgaard
www.margretheodgaard.com
126

Pave Architects
www.pavearkkitehdit.fi
142

Arkkitehtitoimisto Teemu Pirinen
www.teemupirinen.com
178

Primus Architect
www.primus.nu
82

Pushak
www.pushak.no
122, 154

Reiulf Ramstad Architects
www.reiulframstadarchitects.com
54

Arkitekt August Schmidt
www.arkitektaugust.no
100

Tuomas Siitonen Office
www.tuomassiitonen.fi                                        16

Stinessen Arkitektur
www.snorrestinessen.com                                      172

Tham & Videgård Arkitekter
www.thamvidegard.se                                          24, 92

Studio Tolvanen
www.studiotolvanen.com                                       168

Trigueiros Architecture
www.trigueiros.net                                           104, 132

TYIN Tegnestue Architects
www.tyinarchitects.com                                       74

Mork-Ulnes Architects
www.morkulnes.com                                            8

Wingårdhs
www.wingardhs.se                                             50, 158

# Picture Credits

| | |
|---|---|
| Pasi Aalto / www.pasiaalto.com | 74–77, 100, 103 |
| Terje Arntsen | 172, 176–177 |
| Mikko Auerniitty | 117 |
| Austigard Arkitetur AS | 31 |
| Petra Bindel for Muuto | 126–127 |
| Jonas Bjerre-Poulsen | 138–141, 164–167 |
| BoConcept | 150–153 |
| Tia Borgsmidt | 40–43 |
| Kaia Brænne | 88, 90 b. |
| Ivan Brodey | 30, 32–33, 89, 90 a., 91 |
| Arno de la Chapelle, Oulu | 142–145 |
| Bruce Damonte | 8–11 |
| Johan Fowelin | 78–81 |
| Fredericia Furniture | 29 |
| Marc Goodwin / Archmospheres | 34–39, 178–181 |
| Inger Marie Grini, Oslo | 111, 113 a. r., 146–149 |
| Jiri Havran | 154–157 |
| Carl-Viggo Hølmebakk | 182–187 |
| Enok Holsegaard | 28 |
| Hundven-Clements Photography | 20–23 |
| Katri Kapanen | 169 |
| Philip Karlberg / www.philipkarlberg.com, Art Director Anders Nord / www.andersnord.com | 70–73 |
| Steve King | 7, 173–175 |
| Arne B. Langleite | 122–125 |
| Åke E:son Lindman, Stockholm | 24–27, 50–53, 92–95, 104–109, 118–121 |
| Lauri Louekari | 44–49 |
| Mikael Lundblad, Stockholm | 12–15 |
| Kasper Bonna Lundgaard | 128–131 |
| Maija Luutonen, Helsinki | 16–17 |
| Åsa Mikkelsen, Oslo | 101 |
| Muuto | 168, 170 a., 171 b. |
| Normann Copenhagen | 96–99 |
| Nils Petter Dale, Oslo | 110, 112, 113 a. l. |
| Reiulf Ramstad Architects | 54–57 |
| Sameli Rantanen / Asun | 114–116 |
| Marius Rua | 62–65 |
| August Schmidt, Trondheim | 102 |
| James Silverman | 158–163 |
| Laura Stamer / Stamers Kontor and David Bülow | 82–87 |
| Ulf Svane | 59 |
| Jussi Tiainen | 66–69 |
| Chris Tonnesen | 58, 60–61 |
| Trigueiros Architecture | 132–137 |
| Tim van de Velde, Brussels | 18–19 |
| Woud | 170 b., 171 a. |

All other pictures were made available by the architects and designers.
Cover front: Tia Borgsmidt
Cover back (from above to below): Marc Goodwin / Archmospheres, BoConcept

# Imprint

The Deutsche Nationalbibliothek lists this publication in the Deutsche Nationalbibliografie; detailed bibliographic data are available on the Internet at http://dnb.dnb.de.

ISBN 978-3-03768-246-3
© 2019 by Braun Publishing AG
www.braun-publishing.ch

3rd edition 2024

Editor
Editorial Office van Uffelen

Editorial staff and layout
Julia Heinemann, Chris van Uffelen

Graphic concept
Studio LZ, Stuttgart

Reproduction
Bild1Druck GmbH, Berlin